HOVER OVER HER

WICK POETRY FIRST BOOK SERIES

DAVID HASSLER, EDITOR

The Local World by Mira Rosenthal	Maggie Anderson, Judge
Wet by Carolyn Creedon	Edward Hirsch, Judge
The Dead Eat Everything by Michael Mlekoday	Dorianne Laux, Judge
The Spectral Wilderness by Oliver Bendorf	Mark Doty, Judge
Translation by Matthew Minicucci	Jane Hirshfield, Judge
hover over her by Leah Poole Osowski	Adrian Matejka, Judge

MAGGIE ANDERSON, EDITOR EMERITA

Already the World by Victoria Redel	Gerald Stern, Judge
Likely by Lisa Coffman	Alicia Suskin Ostriker, Judge
Intended Place by Rosemary Willey	Yusef Komunyakaa, Judge
The Apprentice of Fever by Richard Tayson	Marilyn Hacker, Judge
Beyond the Velvet Curtain by Karen Kovacik	Henry Taylor, Judge
The Gospel of Barbecue by Honorée Fanonne Jeffers	Lucille Clifton, Judge
Paper Cathedrals by Morri Creech	Li-Young Lee, Judge
Back Through Interruption by Kate Northrop	Lynn Emanuel, Judge
The Drowned Girl by Eve Alexandra	C. K. Williams, Judge
Rooms and Fields: Dramatic Monologues from the War in Bosnia by Lee Peterson	Jean Valentine, Judge
Trying to Speak by Anele Rubin	Philip Levine, Judge
Intaglio by Ariana-Sophia M. Kartsonis	Eleanor Wilner, Judge
Constituents of Matter by Anna Leahy	Alberto Rios, Judge
Far from Algiers by Djelloul Marbrook	Toi Derricotte, Judge
The Infirmary by Edward Micus	Stephen Dunn, Judge
Visible Heavens by Joanna Solfrian	Naomi Shihab Nye, Judge

hover over her

Poems by

Leah Poole Osowski

The Kent State University Press

Kent, Ohio

The Wick Poetry Series is sponsored by the Stan and Tom Wick Poetry Center and the Department of English at Kent State University.

20 19 18 17 16   5 4 3 2 1

For Amara
For arriving

"What will she do after I go? he wonders. Her evening. It closed his breath.
Her strange evening."
    —Anne Carson

CONTENTS

III.

IV.

FOREWORD BY ADRIAN MATEJKA

The poems in Leah Osowski's exquisite debut, *hover over her,* trace the various constructions of adolescence and gender in twenty-first-century America through the experience of three young women who speak in a single, collective voice. That's the easy, catalogue-like description. But the narrative through-line is complicated by the notion of geography: the poems' geographies, the girls' physical spaces, the landscapes of Osowski's lyrical music and syntax. In one way or another, these poems are constantly trying to locate themselves, living in the liminal spaces between comfort and fear, discovery and youth.

It makes sense, then, that the book begins with an epigraph from Anne Carson about locating the self. Place and time are both signifier and totem for this contemporary version of adolescence, where young women—even in a group of three—are singular amidst their cacophonous backdrops. Whether beside a lake, inside a Dali painting, or stretched out in a flower garden, these young women are searching and seeking while also being sought after and regarded.

Osowski's deft lyrical turns make the figures in the poems simultaneously empathetic and mythological, little surrealist paintings where, in the hands of a girl next to a pool, "blue petals twirl like a helicopter rotor hovering over a lake search." All of the poems in the book work this way—with every soft-focus moment, every spinning flower petal foregrounding the dangers to the self and body in our contemporary spaces of forgetfulness and need.

And in illuminating those dangers, they also show us the ways in which we are complicit in the constructions and obstructions of gender. Take, for example, these lines from "she as pronoun":

She thrashes blushes vanishes
wishes on eyelashes for bushels
of sheets to stretch at knee-height
wall to wall in all the unfurnished rooms
to add another level
between floor and ceiling

She's I and she's you every
time you hid beneath your own arms
wrapped across your chest or threw them

into the air and detached they took off
like bottle rockets   Then the clamor and the lit
upturned faces   Sheen
She's off the shelf

    In these lines, the poet not only pushes back against gender and norms, she also (literally) breaks apart postures and body identities. That's where revelations of self, body, and sexuality happen. And while these epiphanies sometimes lead to renaissance in Osowski's collective speaker(s), we more often find that the realizations come from shared affirmation, in connections of memory and collective experiences—of friends, of witnesses, and of sisters in the traumas of growing up in this particular time and space.

    Osowski is a poet who writes with her ears, her heart, and her eyes. Her speakers try to make sense of manifold possibilities in their respective environments, their often blurry geographies of water and fields. It is through their seeking that Osowski is able to find these particular spaces and octaves of language. The end result is a collection of poems that offers both warning and solace, one that leaves you feeling equal parts unsettled and complicit in the geographies we construct and inhabit every day.

ACKNOWLEDGMENTS

Thanks to the editors of the following publications in which versions of these poems first appeared: *The Boiler Journal:* "The Middle Dark," "For the Unrealized Girls"; *Black Warrior Review:* "Moonstone"; *Hotel Amerika:* "Their occurrence," "Words our breaths our bears"; *Mid-American Review:* "controlled burn," "to reach an alternate dimension," "the lakes speak of ice"; *New Delta Review:* "when you swallowed a town"; *Painted Bride Quarterly:* "Salvador Dali—female figure with head of flowers—1937"; *Salamander:* "tied"; *Third Coast:* "Girls with bodies of drawers"; *Weave:* "Salvador Dali—Portrait of Gala—1931."

With my thanks:

to David Hassler and everyone at the Wick Poetry Center and the Kent State University Press for bringing this book to life; to Adrian Matejka for his choice, taste, and trust; to Sarah Messer, Malena Mörling, and Mike White for their immeasurable knowledge; to Sarah & Ananda for our trio—before nostalgia, exists experience; and lastly to John, for every facet, every day, expanding on and on.

I.

THEIR OCCURRENCE

We came in folded bodies in inner tubes
roll downing lawns

    We came calf-bruised
as fell chestnuts   hair clover full   Bled white

  like milkweeds
      Coughing up cotton bolls

We came damp as nightcrawlers
     our restless creek mouths

staining rooms with waterlines   and mellow babbles

We came when we weren't looking

We came to ask you to stay   to never not arrive

Our cricket hearts   have that ascending effect
         on aural landscapes
But what do you call a crescendo
that never breaks

We came to keep climbing   blister heavy handed

   to take the air
      from evaporate

  knock some solid into squander

We came as proof of life and we're holding it plum-heavy

to your ear or lips or eyes you decide

PROPULSION

The girl squats at the lip of the town pool.
She rubs the stem of an aster back and forth
between her fingertips. The blue petals twirl like a helicopter rotor
hovering over a lake search. The tall man standing to the left:
poised at the edge of the deep end. One hand pressed to his chest
as he swings his other arm in a wide circle greasing the joint.
The August air stirs, ripples the chlorine surface as the sun
exits behind the bathrooms. There's a tensing in the muscles
of this place. She stands abruptly, her back to the water, and takes off
arching her small body skywards. There's the escalating
drumbeat on the ear canal that comes from no discernable direction.
And her limbs are petals spinning out from her core.
And the world turns upside down.

SHE AS PRONOUN

She's the scope
between tentacles   the air around
the welt   She will not be soothed
with baking soda and water

She's owl   stingray   ozone
mezzanine   foyer   fog layer
She's baitfishes and shellfires
sheetrock and tarnished

She thrashes   blushes   vanishes
wishes on eyelashes for bushels
of sheets to stretch at knee-height
wall to wall in all the unfurnished rooms
to add another level
between floor and ceiling

She's I and she's you every
time you hid beneath your own arms
wrapped across your chest or threw them

into the air and detached they took off
like bottle rockets   Then the clamor and the lit
upturned faces   Sheen
She's off the shelf

There's a horse the color of rain-heavy chestnut shells that needs to be reined and the ropes staked to the earth. Smell damp, smell soaking, smell matted. Then a hole can be dug in a manner that causes the arms to become vascular and the grip all knuckles. Hear hooves, hear blisters, hear penumbra. Once a depth of seven feet and the width and length of a small barn door is accomplished, place the horse into the ground, upside down on its back, replace the dirt, tamp it solid. Taste parched, taste frantic, taste pupils larger than lakes. When the cantering begins like an earthquake in a closet, lay your back to the heavy stirring soil and wait for something like lightning but a color you've never seen before.

It's like a lynx scratch. Like igniting ethanol-soaked roots. Like being stabbed by an icicle. The sky darkens and speeds up its procession of clouds—hustling them like schoolchildren during a fire alarm. It's like a whip gripped in an outlet, not a hand. Like the opposite of plate tectonics. Like cliff jumping stars. Does it hurt? we ask the sky. During some storms it's like a migraine, or gravelling the palms in a fall, but other times, especially when the lightning is pink, it feels—the sky blushes sunset and whispers—wonderful. Our eyes widen. It's like thinking gunshot then seeing fireworks.

THREE GIRLS AND SOMETHING LIKE
HOVERING ON A HILL IN VERMONT

They'll take more walks in this phase than any other—

the budding years right before driver's licenses

just after boundaries. Steep is also around,

propels them to run down the pavement

to the one-church town shelving grade B dark amber

so thick you'll still notice the tree rings.

Borders of feeder corn and cosmos petals the flush

of deer tongues. The main event of the house:

an unfrosted picture window in the shower.

The pollened cow pond sees the only-just-starting-to-curve

of their pale bellies dressed in Ivory soap

from three acres away and does an underwater somersault,

taking on more afternoon sun. There's homemade

dandelion wine in the top cabinet. A little brother

grasping a fly swatter. A rooster hung from a cypress,

bleeding out in a kill cone. Most of the poplar stairs

lick the girls' bare feet as they lightning past.

FOR THE UNREALIZED GIRLS

Let's mold moats below all their collarbones.
Our hands are always clutching at that clearing

of our bodies anyway. We'll harness
their pulses—the throb that comes the first time

an earlobe is sealed into the envelope of a mouth,
the beating wingspan of an owl under-chest—

make that the surge of water up their banks
which pools in sweat on the indents

of all their see-through ribs. We'll clasp a drawbridge
at their throats to keep out the man hands,

to keep the lies dipped in butterscotch
schnapps from staying too long in the bedrooms of their brains.

Because maybe girls belong in castles in stone dresses.
Why was it always the boys clad in armor and the girls trailing

their fingers over moss and fern and caterpillars
and their pelvises sucking in under the touch of twigs.

Let's keep them in turrets, train them in arrows
and the clash of air.

TURN INTO SOMETHING WITH ROOTS

And slip into a white pine dress. Smooth out
the bluish-green needles and offer some shade.

Walk lightly and hold in the sap.
There's never a tree that's forgotten

to breathe, their leaves always fluid
even when clutter piles the stairs

to the front door. Trees won't hesitate
to use a window. Window exits more often

have someone else waiting on the lawn
in the shadows of the hydrangea.

Someone to offer a shoulder when drainpipes
lack footing. Someone who will unfold

a thin flannel cloth housing small metal
tools—a spile and a corkscrew delicately

applied to the trunk—and tap for syrup
even knowing the tree is not a maple.

THREE GIRLS ON A FARM IN OHIO

Their heads just clear the living lace of dill
in the herb garden, their minds have acres left

to grow. The girl with the softest hands grew up here,
leads the other two across the midsummer fields—

extinguishing their small suburban backyard
with each running arm pump. A toolshed widens

to a barn and a tree branch horse
becomes a bay-colored pony named Moonstone

who they saddle and learn to post and lay hands
on to feel how a blanket can come alive.

Red Hots burn their tongues. They grasp palms
to jump over the fire pit, spit cinders and red ants

across the creek. Underneath matted hair
pillows smell like wood smoke, hay, and window

screens. Soft-Hands stuffs fennel in her pockets
so these cousins will trust her words

which they hold to their chests like kindling.
Still clothed they storm

the aboveground pool, slow run in circles
to create that whirl in the water which sucks

their weightless bodies endlessly around.

GIRLS WITH BODIES OF DRAWERS

salvador dali—city of drawers—1936

Carved not born, these girls are sycamore
and teak. Look at the tree rings circling
up their thighs like bangles, growth seasons

on naked display. The year above the oldest's
left knee, that's when all the rains came
and the trunks turned malleable enough

for them to run across sand-flats
under fireworks and go to bed wet
with too much to drink. Sisters that share

a bedroom, they're a set—dresser and
nightstands untouched by outside
hands, only opened to borrow each other's

dresses. These girls smell of sawdust, a musk
like shavings that line hamsters' cages.
A scent that wants nesting and curled

warm bodies that want
sandpaper massage and secrets buried
in the back corners of underwear drawers:

a catalpa pod hollowed of fiber
holding baby teeth, and a tarot deck
all wands wrapped

in paisley silk. A drawer for a chest
is a chest of drawers is a back and a torso
waist calf and ankle and they've all been

yanked open. Someone broke in their house
ran down the hallway to their room
held his hand over their varnished mouths

so they could only creak like branches
under gusting winds. These girls
must have begged him in shaking leaves

not to finish. Splintering as their possessions
were flung to the floor.
These girls have been ransacked.

It's like falling through all the floors of a ten-story building. Like balls of moonlight. Like running through a sprinkler naked. The knife flashes its metal parts. It's like unlocking a puzzle. Sometimes, if the onion had a bad day, it's like watching a woman completely fall to pieces. Do you cry too? we ask. The knife shakes its blade, My steel is like wearing contact lenses, I'm unaffected. The onions make me feel smart, sharp. I feel in command as they scatter around me. But I always scoop them up with all of my length and let them fall in warm piles into their homes. I introduce them to transforming, and they thank me in sweet smells. So it's the slightest push? we ask. I suppose, the knife responds, all the parts are there, they just need a tour of letting go.

II.

TIED

They were tied, this couple, not knotted—strands looped and holding each other together—but even. Not the even that's caged within revenge, but even like bangs cut straight across a forehead. No stray hairs. They lived at a finish line by the ocean and were always crossing doorways at the same moment. He restored old sailboats and she would stretch the worn canvas masts he removed and paint them with green, orange, and violet. At night they would lie down and line up their parts: her armspan equaled his height and vise versa. On their backs, they'd lay a level across the gap between their hipbones and watch the air bubble slide to the middle. Until the night she woke to the sound of his legs getting longer. Like the moon on a slack tide, there's always something outside, pulling. In the kitchen, she took the lids off the jars of flour and sugar and saw their powders lying at angles. She shook the contents smooth, leaving clouds of dust on the countertop and drifted back to bed. But her searching fingertips only brushed his wrist. She felt lightheaded like he was overusing the oxygen supply in the room with his slow, even breathing. In the morning they sat down next to one another and collected their tears into two tiny bowls. As hers brimmed she looked at his, barely halfway full.

It's like coming home. Like running through a corn maze. Like the Vatican. But it really depends on which side you're in, the blood gushes. If your next stop are the lungs then it feels like you're climbing so many flights of stairs at an area of high elevation. And if you just came from the lungs it's like a dance party in the atrium where nobody ever gets tired and the music is pumping and the energy is so high that the crowd always spills out into the streets and takes to sprinting. It's similar to how scarlet peonies feel to ants or how shells feel to mollusks. What about us? we ask. The blood warms and says, for you it would be like the starting line at a marathon. Ah, we nod and imagine thrumming crowds. And what about love, we ask? The blood gets real quiet. It whispers, we've heard of that version of the heart, we've heard it lives upstairs. And then in a barely audible murmur, like heaven lives upstairs up from you.

LIMINAL

Scrape the residue of hall fire from the laminate floor—an in-between
smoke, like mushrooms puffing spores
or coughs on frozen doorsteps.

Bottle it and watch how clouds pass over a room, dilute the light.

Let a girl drink it and take to pacing,
short of breath.

Picture wildfires in this country that rage in shades of glaucous—
a midpoint between blue and gray—
when flames find trunks, hallways between root and branch.

Know that there are words people don't say to each other,
rectangles of events that hang like smoke in between sentences.
Not because they didn't happen

but because they don't want that hue of oxides
entering the other's eye.

We stood above the tank looking directly down

as stingrays and skates skimmed over one another

Our elbows made acute angles on the ledge

our legs mostly motionless most of them don't stop moving

It's like watching angular Frisbees in slow motion

Stalks of eelgrass broke through the water's surface

out of their atmosphere and into ours

chlorophyll skyscrapers piercing air

(There was one ray paler and stiller than the rest

tones pastel or gas on water)

Rays can shock up to 200 volts

(She lifted off the bottom hovered)

How far of an effecting radius does lightning striking water have?

(A darker ray slid underneath her and rounded the tank)

Could a person keep alive if they dove to the bottom

at that exact post-thunder moment?

(Another ray subtly invaded her abandoned space)

Like sliding down a bench and having the wood feel warmer or colder

Like the way we decide to turn towards or away

from people and temperatures and light

If we were swimming and the sky slashed a blue vein above our heads

depending on our positions treading water

would only one of us die or both?

(They float off from the diamond stirred spot of sand

over the course of several seconds)

THREE GIRLS TREADING ADOLESCENCE

The youngest girl curls inside syllables to pass afternoons
at a private school with no locks on the bathrooms. Her bladder,
a water balloon trying not to break. Her speech, dead-bolted
inside her mouth. Her weekends, vodka so she can catapult
her own boundaries.

Soft-Hands' parents have built a wall in their bedroom to divide
their space. And her brother has painted his four walls black.
She changed one of hers to an orange on mute
and when the cousins visit they brush their teeth on repeat
and drive through snowstorms heat blasting so high they jump
out of the car and dive into an embankment just to breathe.

The oldest girl volleys a ball over a net until her forearms are battered
the purple of frostbite, she sits on the end of a jetty alone.

Summer sleeps them all three in two twin beds pushed together.
The bay at the end of the road draws them daily like deer to a salt lick.
They argue over curfews with their aunts, eat food off of strangers' bussed
plates, compare the thickening callous of their heels and the tongues
of local boys. Eventually they'll get tattoos on their lower backs,
a three-pointed symbol of infinity, but one of them will decide not to
and maybe that's where the distance comes in.

The triangle of attic spanned the length of our slab ranch house under a low-pitch roof. For eighteen years I was terrified to walk hunched under eaves from one end to the other. The middle dark. Like the deep end at the Y. The lights-off hallway between their king bed and our twin bunks. The ceilings at night if you peeled off all my meticulously placed glow-in-the-dark stars. The joints in the pipes that fed the radiators, my father's clicking tarsals muffled by gold-toe black socks. At least four nights a week my dreams are tethered to that gray house with blue window boxes. I can't seem to climb past the gypsy moth tree house, the silver ladder to the porch roof—picking shingles then cherry tomatoes on the patio. I suffocate in lilac bushes and forsythia forts. I'm cornered between rhododendron branches. My flight is limited to the tops of oak trees. My morning mouth tastes like buried acorns, my head the rope swing on the hill—one end chafing bark, the other holding weight, the middle oscillating over a lawn of years.

GLOW STICKS

Phenol and chemistry that excites a dye.
Crack them like taking a frozen lake in your hand,
as a branch, and applying light pressure.
Enter the dark. Teach a girl who's never seen light
held in a tube to throw them toward the ceiling—
see the night split open like fault lines.
Show her to trim her wrist and dance like prisms
in a thunderstorm. Tell her how to keep
them into tomorrow, with tinfoil in the freezer,
and watch her worry. You understand this fear
of losing the light. How many summers did you
break them open over the sands of Cape Cod bay,
shake the chemicals onto the ground to bring
the constellations to your feet? You still taste
the hydrogen peroxide when you kiss strangers.
Still mourn the slow deaths of jarred fireflies,
of sand-covered beach fires, of flashlight beams
spelling your name into space.

AFTER THIS POEM HE WRITES A WISH ON
TISSUE PAPER AND BURNS IT

This boy's color is pitch, it's gray like the skin of South Africans
who've spent months in the diamond mines but he hasn't been
underground he's only stopped wishing for nine years.
And I tell him I think that's like snipping off corners
of electrical tape and blacking out stars or plowing fields
of snow angels or bombing whales and all the rooms in all the houses
that overlook the oceans. And he must think I know nothing
of the body's ability to betray, how an infection can spread
down the Eustachian tube of the ear and claim two major organs
and he's right but I do know that you can't stop asking the space
outside of the envelopes we live in to grant you wishes
because if everyone stopped closing their eyes for a few seconds
and whispering within their mouths the things that would lighten
the color of the light inside their bodies then the earth would
darken to the opaque black of graphite and all the canaries
would drop like hailstones out of the sky.

WHEN YOU INGESTED AN EARTH AND RUINED THE SEASONS

Late August, in the bird's throat
another earth, precisely the size of a beach plum,
ripens and specks of continents
are regurgitated into orbit. *We're the only ones in the world*
you said, *that know*

Spring is coming. Fall unpacked in a tin that smells of shed,
Winter sleepwalking down roads
that dead end at frozen oceans. Spring hovers at brow-level
with the tiny planet you pinch
from the air and grape into your mouth. *I want to taste all the lives*

you say, post swallow.
We call this hour wood-grain, varnish its minutes by hand
as you sweat out the Pacific.
I'm hungry, I say and all the unborn apples come to mind.
I'll never have to eat again

you say. I rest my ear to your throat, hear the harvest
in South America, think about the word *cheat.*

LAKE

You speak in aged hinges
or the silent hiss of eels. Like theirs
your blood is toxic black, anaphylactic.

Your depth is something ravenous:
tornado, hyena.

You locked loch.
Steamer trunk of slick leather.
Taste of castor oil. Your color

like murder, like swarms of swimming
crows. You asthma attack. You ulcer.

SMALL STORMS

there's a hurricane inside the acorn
squash, winds roasting the halls

yellow with warm yells

the saltshaker's a hailstorm

what heavy taste
what weighed-down swallows

you sit on the windowsill
try to assume the lightness of curtains

the invisibility of glass

but the raccoon you ran over
last night just wants to talk

the eggs must be checked for reptiles
snakes separated from the whites

yolks compared in size
to your kneecaps

in strength to your stare

if you were to open the backdoor
the cells of the wasp nest on the frame

would papier-mâché your mouth
and comb through the whole house

AMONG MOTION

Draw the arm back at the elbow
and enter the action of a throw:
the object's breach of the gravity gate
as it takes to the streets of air.

Does the thrown know where it's going
mid-weightless arch? Does it panic?
Are there rocks in the seven countries
that still practice stoning who try to stop—

dragging their granite feet against the floor
in contrails, or shifting their atoms
to vapor so the accused feels airbrushed
instead of battered?

We all begin throwing bubbles with our breath.
We throw water at our faces and yells
from our throats—watch them chug the air
like parachutes and hang over a room.

And this New Year's we held potatoes to our foreheads,
strained the clutter of the last twelve months
out of our memory and wished it into the starch
before launching the vegetables into the sound.

That's when the ear waits for the splash—
same as it waits for a thud, a scream: all sounds of impact.
Like the muffled mouth against a shoulder
when we throw ourselves into each other's arms.

It's like lace. Like a solid layer of fat on soup. Like the opposite of sun-burned skin. It feels like being locked in your room, the lakes say, and stamp their currents. Sometimes the ice feels like eggshells. And when it starts to melt it's like taking a cold shower. Do you have ice? they ask. Not on top of us, we say, but we have ceilings too much of the time. We have down comforters, and scabs. The lakes nod, they know about these things because they live all over the world. When men come, they say, with poles and hooks and lines and cut a hole in it then we feel like whales. But when the children come gliding we think it feels shallow—they stay on our surface instead of diving deep inside of us and letting us wrap them in our green-black arms.

YOUR LACK OF TOUCH

Is stacking igloos. Every time you keep
your hands to yourself, I accumulate a clump
of cold, pack it firmly between the gloved curve
of my palm, mortar another snowbrick.

If hot tap water is run over snow day hands
the temperature is misinterpreted: even the heat
feels freezing. What is this year that refuses
to suck the color back; that's paused the blood flow?

My skin as an ice rink
doesn't want to be resurfaced.
It wants well-worn—deep skate-blade cuts
embedded like white tattoos.
It wants permanent and public displays.

New Englanders staple-gun heavy duty
plastic sheeting to their screened-in porches
to block out six months of winter.
My skin as those backyard screens
loves to stay insulated. How some springs
residents forget to switchblade the wrapping,
staying humid and blurry all summer.

Remember the *carpobrotus,* the ice plants,
that week in San Diego last March?
Their fuchsia-flowered sprawl
of succulent ground cover mulching the highway banks.
Days of wandering with our hands always
clasped between us. And at night, how we'd face each other
sideways under the hotel sheet and hold
the earth together.

MOONSTONE

1. In India moonstone is considered a "dream stone." I've been sleeping with one under my pillow since I was twelve. It makes the tiniest crater in a futon mattress.

2. Specific gravity: 2.61. Luster: opalescent. Streak: white. Mohs scale: 6.0. What if a person was as easily categorized? That scale of minerality would have to be sliding. You hardened in our second year, from gypsum to corundum, or maybe I was just more susceptible to the scratch.

3. You've always lived across the channel. Four and a half hours by car, 239 miles, over seven hours if two ferries are taken. Who decides when the physical distance that exists between two people becomes too far? How do you translate the dialect of miles into the rushing blood flow of the heart?

4. One moon day is 29 ½ days on earth. When you would drive down for the weekend that first year, the few days before became moon days. Turtles and honey and moon snails. Insomnia and the four minutes before a French press can be pressed. That was three years ago and you're still the only person laying varying pressures against my hips.

5. Moonstone is wide white bands of pulled taffy, ribbons of butter in a cream base, under the peel of apples and turnips and daikon root. It's the light, scar-patterned flesh on your abdomen where you were bitten by a brain coral. It's glaciers feeding the Arctic Ocean. It's milk.

6. Holes left in the gums are spaces the tongue likes flitting back to. Holes in the memory of dreams are almost like they never happened. Remembering falling in love with you is both.

7. Regolith is the soil of the moon, its texture like snow and its smell—spent gunpowder. Imagine the explosion. Moon dust blanketing 14.6 million square miles of surface. Was it louder than all the teeth on earth chomping down at the same instant?

8. Samoyeds are the whitest dogs I know. Growing up I had two, two lion manes to bury my face in when I loved them too hard. Samoyeds against the snow are surprisingly yellow.

9. Has the white of cumulous clouds ever been measured against the white of the snow? Or corneas, wave crests, milkweed drops, bathtubs?

10. You think you know the shade of someone once your body has laid next to theirs a certain number of times. But then the question arises— what color, if any, are they when the light goes out?

11. Snow angels in a blizzard.

THE YOUNGEST OF THE THREE GIRLS

Her eyes—mud puddles at noon. Her sleep—
a moonstone under the pillow. She slices radishes
into thin moons during the waxing and waning.
She's a crescent that knows not how to inhabit
her whole. Snob is a shell that houses the shy.

Grape juice a chaser for the vodka invading the house.
The night streets see the youngest lit up. She does this
to find her words, to teach her lips how to kiss, to let
a boy into the circle of air around her body. This

tipped over halo for years. Never not a colt
on thin legs. Never not a voice lost underwater.

The birthmark on her back shaped like Cuba
and she's never not an island. The letters

to and from Soft-Hands lose their frequency
as miles between are added. The faces
they stare into unknown to each other.

The youngest could turn to this current lake
lack of boy and describe her cousins' leopard eyes—
their amber, their wide brow, the whole pollen
covered pond of them—but she can't stand to
see him not care.

What if the time something takes to melt exactly equaled
the time it takes to freeze? How balanced the undoing, the redoing,
or here would you say patching, cure, revival.

Snow would be so much harder its second time around.

Remember snowballs saved in the back of the freezer, how red
the skin of the face turns on impact with thrown ice.

And how red is the human heart that follows that same pattern
of water and frost? The swell periods of liquefying, a new face

in the room, and then the inevitable calcification—
petrified wood, copper in tone.

III.

BECAUSE IT'S JUST FROZEN WATER

I never think about missing snow. That temperature
of my brain has been blotted out.

Yet last December I stayed North for an extra night—
a storm in Madison, Connecticut, powdered my exit
so I borrowed snow pants and gloves like cabins
shared a bottle of champagne through flaked
eyelashes on a padded street. I forgot what it meant
to hate the cold, shuffling tracks in all that thermal,

accumulating cornstarch. Mute night trapped
sound waves between pieces of powder
like being underwater even the way it holds

the body. The ground everywhere was a koozie.
Our dark beer poured onto the white was deer piss
the brown of licked tree trunks. Different
from how urine drills into the sand, or disperses
into the ocean—so quick, the dilution,
something like melting, but even warmer.

Refilled, they'd rock, no wind, a slosh up their sides. Surfaces
blurred gasoline but the boats were all gone, napping under heavy
canvas in driveways and side yards. Soon they stopped reflecting.
They resembled tar pits under hot sun, bitumen only the bravest kids
would swim in, rods and reels hooking bare bones, no light left
for scales. Someone saw two lakes gather up their waters
like bed sheets and switch places, shifting in the new earth
like mattresses of the wrong firmness. The smell those weeks
was restless and skunk, tap water more sulfur than usual.
Babies woke up blue and pruned and colder than resent.
One man drowned in a puddle. Leeches lined the rims of
refrigerator doors and canoes dragged down the highways.
One of the girls who still swam took up talking with the lakes.
She'd open her eyes underwater and see nothing. A sought-after
deprivation. She spoke of dialysis, pointed to small bruises
on her inner bicep. The lakes tuned to her, warmed the waters
where she tread. The girl pricked her finger, let her blood diffuse
into the dark, said *brothers, behave,* and the lakes returned
the color of the sky and exited out the back doors.

THREE GIRLS SUBMERGED

Soft-Hands went west   her water
Pacific   Pit of eastern indigo
snakes   An ocean you don't
turn your back to   Say sleeper
and watch a body disappear

The oldest: Midwest   third
coast of steelhead & trout
Algae blooms it turquoise
A city tattoos its light to the
lakes back   calls her a tramp

The South plucked the youngest
Atlantic broth of quartz   She
stands on the floor   sees
her feet   stands on the water
sees the future   In the corners

of this triangle they float in blank
dark   imagine its high tide at
the bay   their clothes piled
on jetty   their fire stripped
to coals   their hearts unburned

just paper boats folded in
their inflated chests   a sigh
the trade winds that will scatter
them apart   a waterspout
the whip and beat back together

It's like *crème brûlée*—a browning of cream. Or maple syrup warmed from the moist food underneath it. Sweet on the front of the tongue. It's a preservation in amber but we're still beating into tomorrow and the sun let us borrow her kimono so we feel like a dawning Friday. It's like the applause of minks. And the contrast, the skin says, is cartographic. The skin patterns in gooseflesh as it peers under the waistband. It's forming oceans around continents under here, the colors are worldly. Wonder how long it will stay, the skin thinks, paling.

SALVADOR DALI — FEMALE FIGURE WITH HEAD OF FLOWERS — 1937

Does she see with her stamens? Cry in pollen
and bees? A face in the desert

must wilt, but look at her saunter, a swagger
of hips, a leading thigh. Like a mockingbird

chest the curve of her belly,
shoulders dabbed with the scent of stature.

Waterspouts spin from their coasts, cross
prairies when she calls and this man is bending

into fossils following her.
She's the axis

around which he oscillates and she's all
that he sees. Horizon and gauze.

He's a hula hoop at her slender waist,
her turning torque the centripetal force

that keeps him in orbit. A pencil sketch
of a man, all stem. She's front and center

on the wall above my bed and from below
I see the tossed fragments of bone

at her feet, and how easily he could be erased.
She's the type of woman people change

their shirts for. She must be why I wake up
in the middle of every night, and strip

to skin in sheets,
my scalp a sweat fire of blooming asters.

It's like ice on fire. Like dizzy in the woods. Like a collage of all the sweetest insects with the longest legs and battered wings. It's like the possibility in impossibility, the girls whisper, sharp inhale, lowered lashes. Like the shadows of floating maple leaves cast on the bottom of a pool. Like Spanish moss on a trunk, fingers on an inner wrist, lichen. The girls place hands on their chests and let them slide up toward their throats as their thoughts trail. It's like sketching in frost on glass. Like arrows that aim at everything at once. It's like breathing through someone else's fingers as their hand presses over your lips. It's like being smothered in all the beautiful words that all the boys and girls never said to you.

SALVADOR DALI—PORTRAIT OF GALA—
1931

Who do you keep in your conch-shaped heart?
What animals crowd your chambers like a beating

stockyard? You've finger-painted it onto a cardboard
doily with the oiled skin of eggplants;

mixed pigment, water, and yolk
for a fast-drying tempera.

A heart with a handle
to be easily poured, a heart with a koi

for scaled flashes of scarlet, resilient fish
that learn to eat out of hands. Do you

get that close, Dali, to the ones that feed you?
Or are you a locust, always bounding out

of the grass, always migrating
away in a swarm. Maybe you morph

from goat to gull depending on your mood
or the month or the phase

of the moon. Full you fly and new you stand
stock-still on hillsides, balancing.

Flocks and herds and clouds and schools
all for her, your Gala, the blue blood

at the center. Your heart's an ark
and she's steering. It must weigh tons.

THREE GIRLS IN CALISTOGA FOR A LONG WEEKEND

Before the oldest girl's back is divided
by a column of white satin buttons
on a Sunday when she'll repeat loaded words,

the three girls meet in San Francisco and drive north
where the land starts to roll again in lavender beds
and grapevines. They stay in a room with stones

in the shower and strip into bathrobes
the fluff of whipped egg whites.
The morning is fresh-squeezed

grapefruit juice, afternoon is mint leaves
curling ice cubes in narrow poolside glasses.
The air open above the olive trees and under

the water guests swim two lengths and surface
with a bit of exhale left. The girls haven't
been together in a few years. They get naked

in mud baths and hot springs, strip away absence,
color it ravine red with wine. Maybe *apart*
is a gorge of time easily crossed, or maybe

in a clump of days like this—days with a pulse
like a wild animal under human hands—years
are irrelevant units. What matters is this:

the oldest will wife and it will contain her
as she needs to be held; Soft-Hands' middle name
is Morningstar and always will be; and the youngest

will point across their temporary patio as an owl robs
the dusk with its shock-wide wingspan
and none of them will say for sure that it happened.

WHEN THE ENERGY IN YOUR WORDS
CONDENSED INTO MATTER

You said *come here* and the words solidified
into a crepe myrtle chair with two seats
so we sat close and the wood looked naked

You said *orbit* and it did and I did and it was
indiscernible what pushed and what pulled
but it filled up my mouth like mango

You said *sunburn* and my skin got ripe
and the syllables crisped against the air
falling like snow blisters in a heat wave

And when you stopped talking
monsoons for fifteen months
the swipe of windshield wipers

grew tiresome and gray overexerted
But your oral return flipped the sogging
into a Tortola marina where underneath

the power catamarans tarpon circle
the fluorescent cast of nightlights
their sides flash slow silver

And again indiscernible their size
as the water has that effect on things
but comparatively as fish they are huge

SALVADOR DALI—GRADIVA FINDS THE
ANTHROPOMORPHOUS RUINS—1931

She's been called *the woman who walks through walls.* Gunmetal
and wind, sinew of storm clouds.

The buildings across the desert have crumbled: ruined brick
the color of thunder
and lemons. It's hard for a wall to withstand the pressure
of a woman in want.
The smattrande of her atoms rearranging around mortar
as she materializes to the dark
right foreground, to him, man of broken rock. She clings

to his neck like a sling,
like hanging on his every word, like he had scooped her in slate silk
on a gin fresh night
to carry her in a fold to bed, except he didn't. You can't hold things
up with that many holes in your body.

Gone guts and pelvis all air, she eviscerated him.
Tunneled through like slow-motion
bullets, like a vole pushing his parts aside in obsidian
debris. Yet still he bows

his head to meet her as if he donated these slabs—
she asked for bone marrow
and he handed over all his organs. And now like a flagpole
in winter he can't get the taste
of his mouth out of her. He's pushed the limit

of how many electrons
can be offered to another person before all they see
in your face is sky
and sheets of rain. Rilke says, *You who may disappear*
because the other
has wholly emerged. In a matter of days he'll be extinguished

and she'll soar
in the smoke of him to signal in black plumes for another.

REMNANTS

Collect water rings glasses left on tables
to decorate your wrists. Peel fingerprints off objects with a thumbnail,

let them dissolve on your tongue like communion—
taste the opposite of duplicate.

Find a cool window where a forehead took pause
place your ear to the smudge to hear the sigh trapped in glass.

Then listen for muffled patter in the snow and lie
among the rabbit prints, absorb the quickness through your cells

to add another tempo to your bloodstream. Imagine all the laps
you've sat on if every public bench, every classroom chair, still held

the accumulated bodies of their users. Does that rouse your pulse?
Does collecting the translucent make you condensate—sweat stacking,

overflowing rain gauges, runoff in a reservoir
piped to the glasses of thousands of mouths. And how many mouths

have pressed to the mouth of the one you press your mouth to now?
Gather these clouds of residue, but then like wild animals, let them go.

IV.

She drinks water and her mouth is a room
with a window left open.
He knows because he just swallowed
the porch air from her throat.

They speak sealed, mouth-to-mouth
words let in like moths locked
to lampshades.

Words want to bed down, to burrow
in inhales, shift the straw,
knead circles for curling up.

Say *stay* and it does. Say *story*

and his lungs are rushed by the black
bear that stalked the cornfield   chased
her ten-year-old self.

That same bear burrows down
and beds her creek this winter—
its hibernating heart rate a slow climb
of stairs.

When it wakes it will chase him
out of the house of her   because
their pulses don't align—he knows
because she told him, because

her speech is meant to be swallowed,
shut into the den of the body,
kept until the seasons shift
and even then, screened in and leashed.

It took seven days for the changes to churn. Thirst brought a taste of metal and the elevated feeling of climbing water towers. Sheep huddled in your joints, muffled the clicking, and your scars smoothed over like repaved roads. You gave up coffee for rush hour and slept like an abandoned coalmine under the layers of a whole population at rest. Parades were better than sex. But during the heaviest hour, the wax moths and wet lawns, you'd cry out in runaways, nightgowns and backpacks skirting around your corners. Graffiti brought color in the beginning until the tarter came, and infidelities stacked up above your ears in migraine patterns. You lost your hair with the geese. *It's too much* you whispered, shoplifting castor oil and waiting for an evacuation that never came. You tried roller coasters and holding your breath upside down to no avail. On the last Friday of the month you took fire to your house, drank the smoke like a gallon of fresh air until you felt the whole hive of them calm. You apologized with singed lips and asked them to leave. They packed quietly in the night. You were a ghost town by dawn.

TO A KETTLE POND

I met you most times with a curved backbone
flipping under your fresh water to imitate the scoop
of you. How you were melon-balled out of the loam,
one flourish, and then the tadpoles just as round.

If you spoke you'd say *oh* as a cloud moved on
above and let light back in to your shallow
depths. The glint of mica in your skin
never ceases to amaze. I've felt the same

about certain perfectly placed moles—I saw two today,
lined up below the x of a girl's cross-back tank straps,
jewelling her spine with drops of onyx.

Maybe I find you approachable because I can walk
a circle around your whole body's shore
or bisect you with a slow breaststroke.
Or is it because, at your removal

from the ground, you'd look just like the hand-carved
wooden salad bowls I grew up with? You a first course;
you an infant water body. Let geese mistake you
for liquid mercury at 12,000 feet. Let oars knead

your every muscle. Let puddles be freckles
and you be more permanent. An accent to a landscape,
something to be thumbed and admired on the skin.

Her speech would smell of orange rinds.

The night windows would stain the walls
with their shadows, and opened, she'd find
a new sky between rooms. The sky—

heat lightning full, would strike the shy
out of her voice, fulgurites left in sand.
Gravity reduced

to a season. A thing that melts. And snow
unbound by temperature. Flakes to rake
and swim under.

She'd transcribe the current cloud speed
into the stare of someone who deserves her.
Be it fast or slow.

Porch light would be a tree.

Her house—full of containers of lit roots.

And memory a hard object she could take from
a shelf and touch its edges. Be splintered by.

She'd emulate the covalent bond of water,
find the strength in oxygen and hydrogen
and how they hold on to each other like sap
to a trunk.

She'd climb those branches
and dive off into a puddle that oceans
in response to the risk taken

because everything
expands with water and flight.

TRACKS OF SOUNDS

On certain mornings thick tire tracks clutter the shoreline
by the ocean, their pattern
too engaging to be rubber. To be from material
that doesn't migrate or breathe.

My last visit home I heard noises from my mother's bedroom,
like screeching through a thick towel, only slower.
The whales sing me to sleep she said.

Those long lines in the sand are the imprints
of the Humpbacks' spines—how they somersault
down the beach before dawn—translating their songs
into acrobatics.

TAKING ON WATER

I live in a house bordered by water west and east
The channel in front always running sideways   a blue-gray treadmill
The Atlantic at my back always pushing its way forward   a lightly

dressed crowd   If I had two wishes for this landscape: a glacier lake
to my right   to brighten the north   pool splash of ice green   a hot spring
to my left   steam the sheer tights on the southern half of this figure

Then I'd reach a long arm 800 miles up to New England
scoop a handful of snow   Lay it in a tin pie plate and sit
at this table   timing the minutes it took to become water

Not only to add another quality to this element
but so I could enter the water bodies at my borders
for that exact amount of melt time and say:
this is how long it takes for something solid to become you

HER FIRST SWIM IN CLEAR CHLORINE

Carried on a hip into the shallow end,
submerging felt like climbing a willow tree. A soft alive.
Make it a willow tree with cherry blossoms.
Petal smooth hands on all the surfaces
of her legs. The warmth rose up to her neck, a new brand
of long-sleeved. A lapping.

A surface to slap that always yelled back—drops of shouts
stinging her eyes. A color like the sky

finally decided to lay down. Did the unformed
brain wonder if the earth had melted? Did it reel
off a catalogue of all objects now accessible—
picture wading her hands into tree trunks, palming the pulp.

Until her mother blew in her tiny face,
automatic inhale, and they dunked, her first trip
underwater. Everything blurred and all the sharp
edges she'd ever encountered dulled.
It was quieter than she didn't remember.

Did her mind know about whales yet
or how to consider the length of forty minutes?
As seconds passed and her throat began the pull
of wanting air, had she learned the word *resent,* or *lung?*

WHERE THE THREE GIRLS HAPPENED TO LAND A DECADE LATER

Scattered sunflower seeds from a beak thirty feet up.

The oldest girl grows a flax seed version of herself
along her interior wall and dozens of walls on a plot of land
in a neighborhood to keep her family dry. She has glass jars
of macadamias and amaranth flour, a husband stowing promises
in toasted hues.

The girl with the softest hands blows to a bay in the west,
to fog patterns and hills almost perpendicular in slope.
Her bright hours filled with olive trees—that silent tambourine
shimmy of millions of leaves. She seals herself into another
girl at night, murmurs *Fabbit* at her napes,
the quick brown rocks jump over the lazy fog.

The third, the youngest of the girls, is trying to ladder
up the air back to the beak that shelled her. Or she's trying
to formulate the action of living entirely
in the ocean. Not yet partnered she can probe
those open spaces, unjarred and unsealed, until the half
of her that wants cabinets and joint things
tethers her billowing half to the land.

It's like a daylong tug-of-war. Like how you hydrate just to sweat. Like being at the best party of the summer but going home alone. It's like indecision, the ocean says, watching a school of tarpon over its shoulder, or ephempagne—a state of constant flux. Sometimes high tide feels like drowning, and other times it's like climbing a ladder to a roof and sitting for a while. Low tide feels like getting naked and slipping into a bathtub. What about the Bay of Fundy? we ask. The ocean rolls its waves and loses its blue as a cloud passes overhead. Okay, what about spring tides? we ask instead. The ocean smirks, that's when we let our crazies out and try to flood the moon. And you probably want to know about slack tide too right? We raise our eyebrows and nod quickly. Slack tide is naptime. The ocean yawns and gets very still. We retreat slowly down the beach, trying not to leave imprints in the sand.

WHEN YOU NAP IN FLOWERBEDS

It will start with a front yard, with a bed
of white and purple pansies
that beg you to lie down among them

as you pass. Hundreds of oxfords
with inkblot stains on the breast pocket.
Cotton, machine-washable, tumble-dry in dew.

They're tiny albino lions with black eyes, pawing at you
to nap with them. *You can't crush us,* they hum in petal,
we're a pack. It'll be like folding into a fur coat

or turning your face
toward the softest hand you've ever felt—
palm like dough kneaded for days. It'll be like Dorothy,

like opium, like downpours on thin roofs. Sleep
where your body never moves and eyes open
from a white soundproof room with no memory.

There will have to be someone behind you, to breathe
against. To calf-stack. To say, don't wake me when it's time
to go I have to water the lions.

Lay beside the lawn, close your eyes and wait
for the space behind your lids to expand into an entrance
hall of an ornate museum. It's called viskava,

the foyer to sleep where you're looking up at high ceilings
with wishbone beams. Hear the children
playing "violet war," how they intertwine the hooks

where the pansy blossoms meet the stems and attempt
to pull the two flowers apart. Whoever's left with more
head is proclaimed the winner. Feel yourself stir

in that wishing place as outside tap-dances across
your cortex, each passing car morphs into another
pride member, roaring across the dusk.

Tonight you're crepuscular, a nomad
in the neighborhood, tomorrow maybe crocuses
or cosmos if you're lucky, if you hold the larger head.

It's like garden gloves. Like Magic Mountain, or any pitch black for a full minute roller coaster. Like cake. The worms wiggle, open and close their tiny worm mouths in agreement. The earth feels like basement sleepovers in flannel-lined sleeping bags. Like weaving through a crowd on a humid night. Like moss in the tree trunks in the forest that have fallen and are now hollow and musk. It feels like the total content that comes with being alone. Or like fingers in between toes. And when it rains it's like an evacuation with no shelters, but instead of panicking we teach ourselves how to swim. Does it ever feel suffocating? we ask, as we think of our dead. No, they reply, it's like sleeping with the covers over your head—there's always enough air somehow.

GATHER HER

The one with the moat necklacing her throat
and the one with the head of asters. Hover
there so she doesn't drown in her own skin
or lose sight among all that stem. Her

in there and here and other, always around.
Cherrystones inherited by a gravel footpath.

So hover over her who wraps herself in lake ice
and her who buries her face in lichen. Hover
so she won't suffocate. Take the her
out of smother, let oxygen back in to the blue

and leave the hurt—that's not even her. Hover
when she swallows towns, takes too many
electrons, and backflips off edges. Suspended
near does not mean intervene, there is no point

of contact. They may be herringbone underneath
but these hers are vibrating at frequencies
above 20,000 hertz. They don't need concern
in fluttering hands. Levitate long enough

and she'll imitate, maneuver her chest
of drawers off their slides and invent another
orbit. These girls never craved to stay
on the ground. They're thermal and feather.

So hover like a light-handed gravity and keep
them in atmosphere. They look so good
noosed up in nitrogen with a thin callous
to their feet. It's not that they shouldn't float

to other worlds, hermit in ether, we just don't
want to lose them yet. Because her plus at equals:

they adhere to ours, this herd of hers
yellow-crowned night herons
foot stirring our hearts, like hidden fiddler crabs,
out of the wetland.